Date Due

NOV 13 2014			

BRODART, CO.   Cat. No. 23-233   Printed in U.S.A.

ARCHAEOLOGICAL MYSTERIES

SECRETS OF
MACHU
PICCHU

LOST CITY OF THE INCAS

BY SUZANNE GARBE

Consultant:
Linda Olson
Professor of Humanities
Minot State University
Minot, North Dakota

CAPSTONE PRESS
a capstone imprint

Edge Books are published by Capstone Press,
1710 Roe Crest Drive, North Mankato, Minnesota 56003
www.capstonepub.com

Library of Congress Cataloging-in-Publication Data
Garbe, Suzanne.
Secrets of Machu Picchu : lost city of the Incas / by Suzanne Garbe.
    pages cm.—(Edge Books. Archaeological mysteries)
Includes bibliographical references and index.
Summary: "Describes the archaeological wonder of Machu Picchu, including
discovery, artifacts, ancient peoples, and preservation"—Provided by publisher.
ISBN 978-1-4765-9919-9 (library binding)
ISBN 978-1-4765-9928-1 (pbk.)
ISBN 978-1-4765-9924-3 (ebook pdf)
1. Machu Picchu Site (Peru)—Juvenile literature. 2. Inca architecture—Juvenile
literature. 3. Peru—Antiquities—Juvenile literature. I. Title.
F3429.1.M3G37 2015
985'.01—dc23   2014006971

Developed and Produced by Focus Strategic Communications, Inc.
    Adrianna Edwards: project manager
    Ron Edwards: editor
    Rob Scanlan: designer and compositor
    Karen Hunter: media researcher
    Francine Geraci: copy editor and proofreader
    Wendy Scavuzzo: fact checker

Photo Credits
Alamy: GL Archive, 23 (top); Corbis: National Geographic Society/Hiram Bingham,
5 (top); Courtesy of Lyndsey Clark, 18–19; Courtesy of the Division of Anthropology,
American Museum of Natural History, 14; Deborah Crowle Illustrations, 6, 25; Getty
Images: Gordon Wiltsie, 13, The Bridgeman Art Library, 24; iStockphoto: mcwhitey,
12, mirc3a, 26–27, wayra, 3, 7; Newscom: Danita Delimont Photography/Keren Su,
17 (bottom); Shutterstock: Dr. Morley Read, 4–5, ene, 8, Hailin Chen, 20–21, Jarno
Gonzalez Zarraonandia, cover, 1, kccullenPhoto, 11, Mariusz S. Jurgielewicz, 8–9
(back), 22–23 (back), Ralf Broskvar, 29; Thinkstock: Ostill, 9; Wikipedia: McKay
Savage, 28, Neal Grout, 17 (top), Ragesoss, 15

Design Elements by Shutterstock

Printed in the United States of America in Stevens Point, Wisconsin
042014   008092WZF14

TABLE OF CONTENTS

CHAPTER ONE

A REAL-LIFE
INDIANA JONES

By day Hiram Bingham III worked as a history professor. But outside the classroom, he was a man on a mission. The world would soon know him as an explorer and an adventurer.

Bingham was known mostly for his fascination with Latin American history. Then in 1911 he organized an **expedition** to Peru. He knew the country's thick jungle hid lost cities and secrets. One of those secrets was the fortress where the native Incas had their last battle with Spanish invaders. Bingham knew this would be an important discovery—if he could find it.

expedition—a journey with a goal, such as exploring or
searching for something

BINGHAM'S "DISCOVERY"

Most people say that Hiram Bingham "discovered" Machu Picchu. But Machu Picchu couldn't really be discovered because Peruvians always knew it was there. Today when someone says that a person "discovered" a place, it sometimes means that the person rediscovered the place and made it famous. This more informal definition holds true in the case of Bingham "discovering" Machu Picchu.

Hiram Bingham

ARCHAEOLOGICAL FACT

In the Incan language, Machu Picchu means "Old Mountain" or "Old Peak." The large peak that towers over Machu Picchu is Huayna Picchu. This means "Young Peak" or "Young Mountain."

5

THE INCAN EMPIRE

The Incan Empire was the biggest **empire** ever to exist in either North or South America. At its height, it stretched about 2,500 miles (4,000 kilometers) along the west coast of South America. This is almost as long as the United States is wide. The empire included parts of modern-day Peru, Colombia, Bolivia, Chile, Argentina, and Ecuador.

empire—a large territory ruled by a powerful leader

The Incan Empire was the largest of its kind in the Americas before the arrival of Europeans in 1532.

SOUTH AMERICA

Machu Picchu

Lima

Cuzco (Inca Capital)

La Paz

PACIFIC OCEAN

Incan Empire, 1532

| 0 | 300 | 600 mi |
| 0 | 500 | 1,000 km |

FINDING MACHU PICCHU

After Bingham arrived in Peru, a local farmer told him about some ruins. Following the farmer's directions, Bingham's group climbed up a mountain ridge. The snow-capped peaks of the Andes surrounded them. Suddenly Bingham was staring at a huge maze of white stone buildings partially hidden by the jungle. Bingham realized they might be the most impressive ruins ever found in Peru. He had found not the Incan fortress, but rather Machu Picchu. This discovery made Bingham famous. Many historians now call him a "real-life Indiana Jones."

Machu Picchu

CHAPTER TWO

BUILDINGS
AND RELICS

Hiram Bingham was the first researcher to study Machu Picchu. But he wasn't the last. Many historians, **archaeologists**, and other scientists have visited Machu Picchu. They want to learn about the South American natives, known as Inca, who lived there. The Inca didn't have a writing system, which is why they didn't leave behind any documents. The best clues about their lives come from **artifacts**.

archaeologist—a scientist who studies how people lived in the past by analyzing their artifacts

artifact—an object used in the past that was made by people

Machu Picchu artifacts

No one knows for sure why Machu Picchu was built or what it was used for. The grand construction suggests that it was probably built for rich and powerful people. One theory is that Machu Picchu was a vacation estate for the Incan emperor Pachacuti. Machu Picchu was likely built in the 1450s during Pachacuti's rule.

The site contains about 200 buildings. They were built of stone in the Incan style. Workers carefully cut the stones to fit together so precisely that they did not need masonry. Granite stone was carved to build the walls, stairs and walkways, and the drains and canals that still exist today.

Pachacuti ruled the Incan Empire from 1438 to 1471.

BUILDINGS

One section of the site contains houses. The houses at Machu Picchu have different layouts and decorations. Some of the houses have polished walls that are carved with great detail. This design shows that these houses were built for upper-class people. They are twice as large as houses believed to be used by servants.

Another section of Machu Picchu contains buildings used for **ceremonies**. The Principal Temple has an enormous altar made of granite. Another temple is known as the Temple of the Sun. The floor of the temple is carved with a straight line. It points to the exact direction where the sun rises on the June **solstice**.

ceremony—special actions, words, or music performed to mark an important event

solstice—one of the two days of the year when the sun rises at its northernmost and southernmost points

ARCHAEOLOGICAL FACT

Machu Picchu is now one of the most famous places in South America. But it is not a large place. Historians believe it housed no more than 500 to 750 people.

the Temple of the Sun

EVERYDAY ARTIFACTS

Many everyday artifacts found at Machu Picchu are made of pottery. These include jars, bowls, and plates that are red, black, and cream. Ceramic whistles were also found. Maybe the Inca used these to warn people of intruders or to provide music. Or perhaps they used these in ceremonies. An even bigger mystery are the small pieces of pottery that are marked with a variety of lined patterns. Maybe these were a sort of dice game. Or perhaps these objects were used for worship or as counters in trading goods.

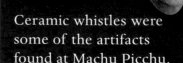

Ceramic whistles were some of the artifacts found at Machu Picchu.

Metal objects were also recovered at Machu Picchu. These include silver pins used by women to keep their shawls closed. Other objects found include bells, mirrors, tweezers, needles, tools, and weapons.

The Inca also made objects of bone and wood. Archaeologists found flutes and weaving tools made from bone. The weaving tools were used by Incan women. The women made cloth that was some of the finest in the world at that time.

Not many wooden objects survived at Machu Picchu. The weather probably destroyed most of these long before Machu Picchu was ever studied.

Incan pins, known as *tupus*, were used to fasten clothing.

ARCHAEOLOGICAL FACT

Machu Picchu is a very wet place. Every year it gets more than 78 inches (198 centimeters) of rainfall.

WEAPONS AND TOOLS

There is no evidence to suggest that Machu Picchu was a military fortress or a place of war. But some weapons were found there. Bingham's group discovered two stones. These were ground into smooth, round shapes, with grooves etched into their centers. This could mean that leather was once tied around them. These were most likely bola stones. Historians believe that the Inca threw bola stones at the legs of enemies and animals to trip and catch them.

Other weapons found at Machu Picchu are made of metal. The head of a **bronze** mace was found there. It was once attached to a wooden handle. Bronze knives and axe heads were also found. They were used as either weapons or tools.

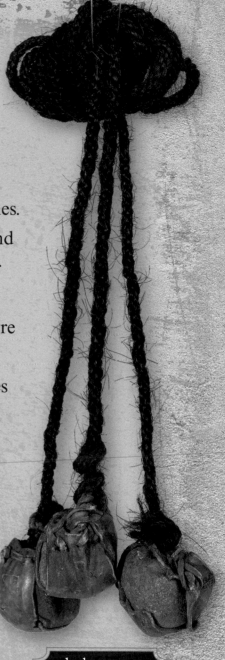

bola stones

bronze—a metal made of copper and tin; bronze has a gold-brown color

WHO OWNS MACHU PICCHU'S ARTIFACTS?

Bingham brought several thousand pieces of metal, ceramic, and bone back to Yale University. The Peruvian government and Yale spent the next century arguing about who owned the objects. Finally, in 2010, an agreement was reached. Two batches of artifacts were returned to Peru in 2011. Most of the rest were sent back in 2012. Yale now works with a Peruvian university to care for the artifacts. Yale also helped Peru organize a touring exhibit of the artifacts.

The Peabody Museum of Natural History at Yale University stored the artifacts that Hiram Bingham sent back from Machu Picchu.

ARCHAEOLOGICAL FACT

One knife found at Machu Picchu has a unique curved blade. Scientists believe it was made to be worn as a pendant. This design is not typical for the region. Historians believe these objects show that people from other cultures came to Machu Picchu from far away.

CHAPTER THREE

PEOPLE

The Incan Empire stretched across South America. In 1438 under Pachacuti's rule, the empire began to grow. The Inca had a strong military force, and they conquered new land. Their main weapons were clubs, axes, and slingshots. Perhaps the axes found at Machu Picchu were once used in battle.

There was nothing unusual about Incan fighting methods. Instead, their greatest skills were their organization and construction work.

The Inca built many roads that allowed them to move and communicate quickly across their empire. These roads helped them to control the land they conquered. One of these roads is the famous Inca Trail. It is the original road that the Inca used to travel between Cuzco and Machu Picchu. It takes three to four days to walk the trail. Incan royalty probably were carried by **litter**.

litter—a hand-carried couch with poles on each side used to transport one person

The Incan military used weapons such as the sling.

Incan royalty often traveled by litter, as shown in this modern re-enactment of the Festival of the Sun. This ceremony is performed every year in June in Cuzco, the Incan capital. It attracts thousands of tourists and local visitors.

MASTERS AND SERVANTS

Historians don't believe the royal family lived year-round at Machu Picchu. The graves found at the site are not those of rich people. The graves were simple. They probably held the bodies of servants who kept Machu Picchu running year-round. Often the graves were just rocks piled around a body. And they contained only a few, well-worn objects such as pieces of pottery. Even fairly poor Inca were often buried with twice that number of objects. The Inca were buried with objects because they believed they would need them in the afterlife.

WHAT BONES TELL US

Archaeologists study skeletons of ancient people to learn about their diet and lifestyle. Skeletons found at Machu Picchu reveal that the people were generally healthy. The main food in their diet was corn. Small pots found there suggest that most cooking was done for a single person or small families.

Although farmland surrounded Machu Picchu, no farming tools were found there. Probably no farmers lived at Machu Picchu itself. However, archaeologists found tools used to create metal. They also found spindles and weaving tools, which suggest that cloth was being made. Unfinished stone carvings suggest that stonemasons lived there. The people living full-time at Machu Picchu were probably a mix of servants and skilled craftspeople.

Archaeologists believe that the people who lived at Machu Picchu came from all over the Incan Empire. The empire was large, and it included many different cultural groups. Scientists think that the variety of pottery found there proves this belief. Recovered human bones show that some of the people possibly ate a lot of fish. This discovery suggests that these people came from a faraway coast.

Grave robbers plundered many Incan tombs and then left them open.

ARCHAEOLOGICAL FACT

The land around Machu Picchu has been farmed for more than 1,000 years without a break.

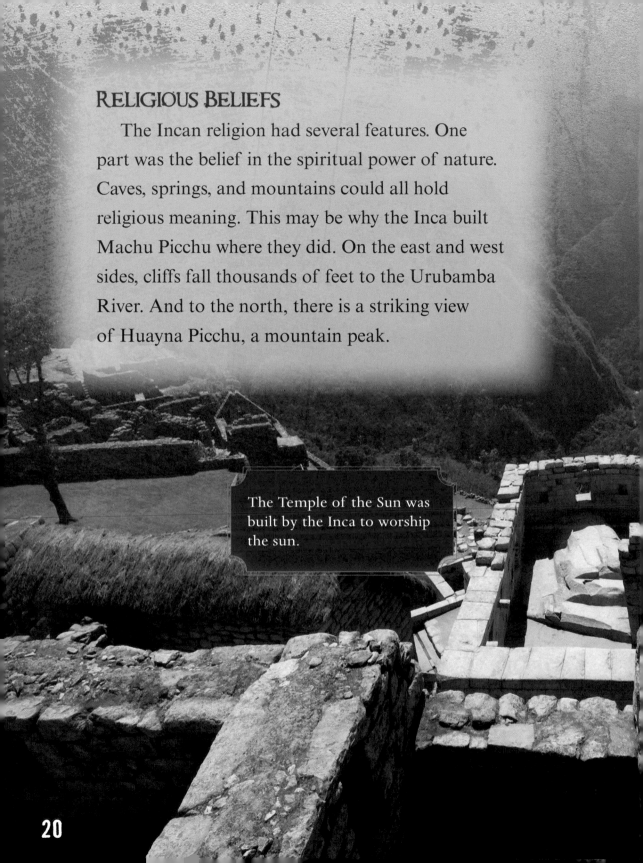

Religious Beliefs

The Incan religion had several features. One part was the belief in the spiritual power of nature. Caves, springs, and mountains could all hold religious meaning. This may be why the Inca built Machu Picchu where they did. On the east and west sides, cliffs fall thousands of feet to the Urubamba River. And to the north, there is a striking view of Huayna Picchu, a mountain peak.

The Temple of the Sun was built by the Inca to worship the sun.

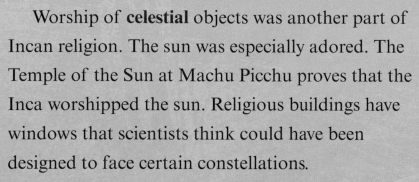

Worship of **celestial** objects was another part of Incan religion. The sun was especially adored. The Temple of the Sun at Machu Picchu proves that the Inca worshipped the sun. Religious buildings have windows that scientists think could have been designed to face certain constellations.

Worship of the royal family was another part of the Incan religion. The Inca believed the royal family was holy. That helped the royal family hold power over their empire.

celestial—relating to the stars and the sky

ARCHAEOLOGICAL FACT
Machu Picchu has more religious buildings than other locations believed to be Incan royal estates.

CHAPTER FOUR

DOWNFALL

The reason why the Incas abandoned Machu Picchu has been called a great mystery. Many historians and archaeologists have guessed why it was abandoned. Lucy Salazar is an expert on Incan archaeology. She is also a former **curator** of Machu Picchu artifacts at the Yale University Peabody Museum of Natural History. She thinks the reason is fairly simple.

According to Salazar, if Machu Picchu was Pachacuti's estate, it was a place for wealthy people. It was in a remote setting. Only a wealthy empire could support such a place for its ruler. When Pachacuti built Machu Picchu, the Incan Empire was rich. But that wealth did not last forever.

The Incan emperors after Pachacuti continued to expand the empire, but there were **rivalries**. In the late 1400s Huayna Capac became the new ruler. He expanded the Incan Empire to its largest size yet.

But Huayna Capac died suddenly around 1525 and named no **heir**. Two of his sons, Atahuallpa and Huáscar, fought to become the new king. After years of fighting, Atahuallpa won. The year was 1532—and he faced his empire's biggest threat.

Atahuallpa

ARCHAEOLOGICAL FACT

The Incan main language was called Quechua. Quechua is still spoken widely in Peru today by descendants of the Incas.

curator—a person in charge of the care, display, and preservation of objects

rivalry—a fierce feeling of competition between people or groups

heir—someone who has been or will be left a title, property, or money

descendant—a person who comes from a certain group of ancestors

The Spanish Invasion

Atahuallpa wasn't the only person who wanted control over the Incan Empire. So did the Spanish. Francisco Pizarro, a **conquistador** from Spain, arrived in Peru in 1532. Atahuallpa was traveling to Cuzco to be declared king when he learned that Pizarro wanted to meet with him. Atahuallpa agreed, never suspecting the meeting was a trap. When he entered the meeting space, the Spanish kidnapped him. They demanded money.

conquistador—a military leader in the Spanish conquest of
    North and South America during the 1500s

Francisco Pizarro captured and killed the Incan Emperor Atahuallpa, leading to the end of the Incan Empire.

PIZARRO'S ROUTE THROUGH SOUTH AMERICA

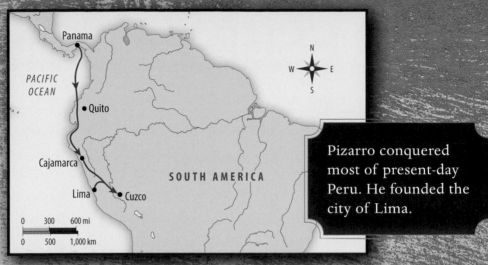

Pizarro conquered most of present-day Peru. He founded the city of Lima.

According to legend, the money the Spanish demanded was three rooms filled with gold and silver. The Incan people brought as much gold and silver to the Spanish as they could. Then the Spanish killed Atahuallpa. They replaced him with a new leader they could control. This led to the downfall of the Incan Empire.

After Atahuallpa was killed, Machu Picchu was used for only a few decades more. After the Incan Empire collapsed, the rulers didn't have the power or wealth to support Machu Picchu. It was too remote for people to stay there without support. Time and nature hid the estate beneath trees, moss, and vines. And there it lay for centuries, known only to the few Peruvians farming in the area.

CHAPTER FIVE

PRESERVATION

Many Incan ruins, including Machu Picchu, are in danger today. **Looters** dig up many artifacts from Incan sites. They often steal these objects at night and don't care what they destroy in the process. They sell the artifacts to foreign countries. As a result, the artifacts are lost to Peruvian history. Even if the artifacts are recovered, archaeologists aren't always able to learn much from them. Knowing where an artifact was found and what was found near it is very important to understanding the item's purpose.

Another threat is tourism. In the early days, few tourists visited Machu Picchu. But more and more people wanted to see the site, and the number of visitors soared. Experts worry that the tourists could end up wearing down the structure.

looter—a person who steals, especially large numbers of things from one place

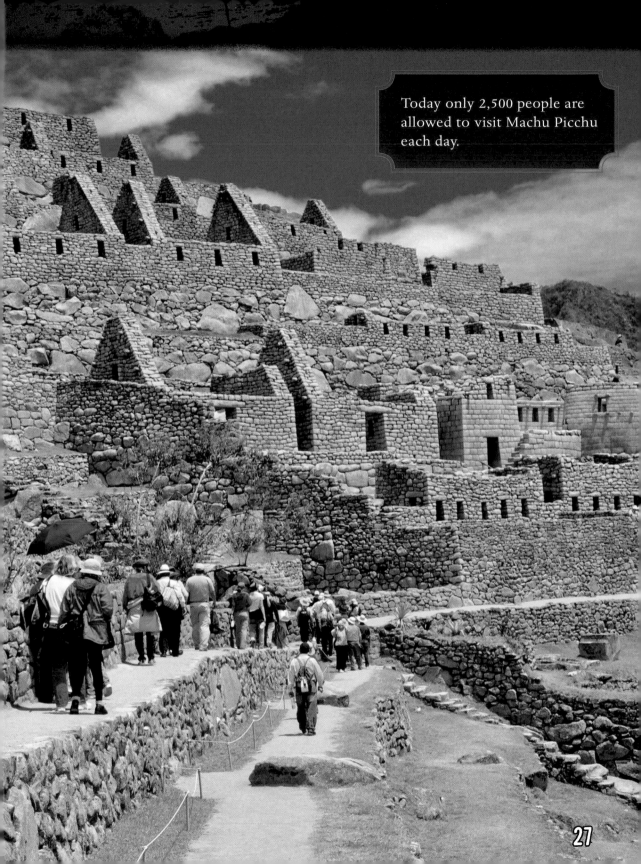

Today only 2,500 people are allowed to visit Machu Picchu each day.

Saving Machu Picchu

Although Machu Picchu faces risks, there are also many people and organizations working to protect it. One organization is the United Nations Educational, Scientific and Cultural Organization (UNESCO). In 1983 UNESCO granted Machu Picchu the title of World Heritage Site. They give this label to natural and human-made places that are "of outstanding value to humanity." UNESCO encourages countries to protect World Heritage Sites. It provides training and money to preserve the sites. UNESCO's money has been used for repairing damage and creating a conservation plan at Machu Picchu.

Preserving Machu Picchu will allow people from around the world to continue visiting the site.

Archaeologists and historians will be able to continue studying Machu Picchu to learn more about the Incan Empire. While modern archaeologists have helped solve some of Machu Picchu's mysteries, many more still remain.

Tourists and earthquakes caused damage to Machu Picchu.

GLOSSARY

archaeologist (ar-kee-AH-luh-jist)—a scientist who studies how people lived in the past by analyzing their artifacts

artifact (AR-tuh-fact)—an object used in the past that was made by people

bronze (BRAHNZ)—a metal made of copper and tin; bronze has a gold-brown color

celestial (suh-LES-chuhl)—relating to the stars and the sky

ceremony (SER-uh-moh-nee)—special actions, words, or music performed to mark an important event

conquistador (kon-KEYS-tuh-dor)—a military leader in the Spanish conquest of North and South America during the 1500s

curator (KYOO-ray-tur)—a person in charge of the care, display, and preservation of objects

descendant (di-SEN-duhnt)—a person who comes from a certain group of ancestors

empire (EM-pire)—a large territory ruled by a powerful leader

expedition (ek-spuh-DI-shuhn)—a journey with a goal, such as exploring or searching for something

heir (AIR)—someone who has been or will be left a title, property, or money

litter (LIT-ur)—a hand-carried couch with poles on each side used to transport one person

looter (LOOT-ur)—a person who steals, especially large numbers of things from one place

rivalry (RYE-val-ree)—a fierce feeling of competition between people or groups

solstice (SOL-stis)—one of the two days of the year when the sun rises at its northernmost and southernmost points

READ MORE

Lewin, Ted. *Lost City: The Discovery of Machu Picchu*. New York: Puffin, 2012.

Newman, Sandra. *The Inca Empire*. True Books: Ancient Civilizations. New York: Children's Press, 2010.

Sohn, Emily. *Investigating Machu Picchu: An Isabel Soto Archaeology Adventure*. Graphic Expeditions. North Mankato, Minn.: Capstone Press, 2010.

CRITICAL THINKING USING THE COMMON CORE

1. Read the first two paragraphs on page 22. Do you agree with Lucy Salazar's opinion of why Machu Picchu was abandoned? Why or why not?
(Craft and Structure)

2. Machu Picchu has been considered "a place of outstanding value to humanity" by UNESCO. What does this mean? Use evidence from the text to show your understanding of the phrase. What would you consider places of outstanding value to citizens of the town in which you live? (Key Ideas and Details)

3. Reread pages 26–29 and think about the effect of tourism. List the problems caused by visitors. Now list the reasons why tourists *should* come to Machu Picchu. Choose a side. Write a persuasive piece stating why people should or should not visit Machu Picchu. (Integration of Knowledge and Ideas)

INTERNET SITES

FactHound offers a safe, fun way to find Internet sites related to this book. All of the sites on FactHound have been researched by our staff.

Here's all you do:

Visit *www.facthound.com*

Type in this code: 9781476599199

Super-cool stuff!

Check out projects, games, and lots more at
www.capstonekids.com

INDEX